Sequence of Events

A Play

George MacEwan Green

A SAMUEL FRENCH ACTING EDITION

SAMUEL FRENCH

FOUNDED 1830

SAMUELFRENCH-LONDON.CO.UK
SAMUELFRENCH.COM

CHARACTERS

Hangman

Claude Vole

Herbert Vole, Claude's father

Margaret Vole, Claude's mother

Lily-Ann Turbett, a prostitute

The action of the play takes place in a railway station waiting room; a prostitute's room and the Vole household

Period : Edwardian

SEQUENCE OF EVENTS

The stage is divided into three separate portions. At R. is a railway
station waiting room, indicated by a wooden bench seat. C.S. is a
prostitute's room, indicated by a rickety table covered with a gaudy
fringed cloth and on the table a cracked swivel mirror. Also at C.S.
are a couple of plain chairs. At L. is a room in the VOLE house,
indicated by a small round table flanked on either side by Edwardian-
style dining chairs. The table is covered with a velveteen cloth and on
it are a bible, a bottle of brandy and two glasses.

The period is Edwardian.

When the play opens, LILY-ANN, in a state of undress, is lying face
down C.S., her arms outstretched. She is absolutely motionless. At
R. HERBERT VOLE, his shirt sleeves rolled up, sits with one elbow on
table, head resting on his hand.

HERBERT	(very quietly) Oh my boy, my boy.
	(HANGMAN enters R. He carries a Gladstone bag and wears a bowler hat. Across his chest is a gold watch chain. He goes to bench and sits down, placing bag at his feet. He removes his hat and, taking a handkerchief from his trouser pocket, wipes the inside band.)
HANGMAN	By Jove, it's warm. I'm sweating like a pig. (He returns handkerchief to pocket, puts bowler back on.) Good weather for trade, though. In my capacity as Publican, I mean. Marvellous good drinking weather this. My word, yes.
	(MARGARET enters L. Her dress has been left open at the neck, her hair hangs down in a

(pigtail. She stands staring at HERBERT.
HERBERT looks up at her.)

HERBERT

Margaret, you should stay in bed.

MARGARET

Should? I won't be told should by anyone.

HERBERT

You know what the doctor said.

MARGARET

I know what he didn't say, as well.

HERBERT

Margaret, be sensible.

(He rises and approaches her, putting out a hand
as if to support her but she shrugs him off.)

Margaret.

MARGARET

Leave me be, Herbert, leave me be.

(MARGARET sits. HERBERT shakes his head
sadly and then also sits.)

What time is it?

HERBERT

About half past seven.

MARGARET

Oh Jesus, my child!

(HANGMAN takes watch from his pocket and
consults it.)

HANGMAN

Half past ten. I'll be home in good time for
lunch. Veal and ham pie, brussel sprouts and
lashings of mashed taters. Thank God, I've an
appetite as will do it justice.   (He returns
watch to his pocket and pats pocket.)   A very
fine, reliable timepiece that. Was my father's
afore me, rest his bones. A pretty face and a
sweet little voice has that watch.

(HERBERT pours from bottle into the two glasses.
He passes a glass to MARGARET. She shakes
her head.)

HERBERT

My dear, you should. Just a sip. It will do you
good.

MARGARET

Good? Are you so slow, so dull-witted, so

useless and worthless that you cannot see that
nothing will ever do me good again as long as I
live?

(HERBERT sips brandy, his hand visibly shaking.)

HANGMAN   After lunch I'll snooze on top of the bed for half
an hour or so. Then when I wake I'll call Sarah
to me. I always want to - need to - on such
occasions. Strange. It was the same with my
father. He told me so when he was a very old
man and tottering on the brink of his dotage. 'Do
it make you randy, lad?' he asked and I said,
'Yes, it do, Pa.' 'Took me the same,' he said.
'One morning I did three - one woman, two men,
all poisoners - and that very afternoon you was
conceived, lad. I begat you on your mother that
very afternoon. The way I felt,' he said, 'with
the beating and pounding in my thighs, I could
have begat a whole regiment.' He was on the
brink of his dotage, or he would never have
spoken of it.

MARGARET   In the attic there's a trunk with his baby shoes
and his shawl, the one my sister crocheted for
his christening.

HERBERT   Yes, I remember.

MARGARET   And there are some crayon drawings he did when
he first went to school. A ginger tomcat sitting
on a mat in front of a huge fire.

HERBERT   Yes, yes.

MARGARET   But what else is there? There must be more than
that. I must have more of him than that.
(As if on impulse, she rises and takes a step
forward and then stops.)   There are photographs, of course.   (She looks at HERBERT
and laughs unsurely.)   There are photographs,
aren't there, Herbert? They're not just images
in my mind?

HERBERT   There are photographs, my dear.

MARGARET   Yes. Good. If they were just in my mind I
                  might forget them - misplace them, lose them.

HERBERT   Why don't you go back to bed, Margaret?

MARGARET   (sitting down)   I'm all right.

HANGMAN   At such times Sarah enjoys it, too. Normally
                  she isn't all that keen. Naturally, respectable
                  women don't have the same taste for it. Sarah
                  does her duty, but she'd never dream of making
                  the first move and I know she's glad when it's
                  over. But when I come home to her after doing
                  this job, she's - she's - well, frankly, she's in
                  heat and although she waits until I call for her,
                  she don't pretend to hide her eagerness.

                  (MARGARET rises and goes D.S. She makes a
                  gesture as if slightly pulling aside a curtain.)

HERBERT   Don't look out, Margaret.

MARGARET   Don't look out on a living world, do you mean?
                  How quiet it is. Is it always so at this time of
                  day? All these houses, all these windows and for
                  all these people it's just another ordinary day.
                  Nothing is touching them. They're safe and snug
                  and without pain.

HANGMAN   Everything went well, everything was quite in
                  order and highly satisfactory. From a technical
                  point of view, I mean. The success of the drop
                  lies mainly in an accurate assessment by myself
                  of the subject's height and weight. I suppose it
                  could be described as scientific or, perhaps,
                  mathematical. However, I feel that with me
                  there's a certain vital degree of intuition involved.
                  I inherited that trait from the old man. I would
                  like to think that before I retire I might be as
                  efficient and capable as he was.

MARGARET   (turning to look U.S.)   I should have begged an
                  audience of the king.

HERBERT   Margaret, Margaret!

HANGMAN   I've only ever botched it once - what you might say
                   really botched it. It was a woman, too. She
                   deceived me properly. Some of the others
                   present was quite put out that it wasn't as swift
                   and clean as it should have been, but, for myself,
                   I couldn't help feeling grieved against the
                   woman that she had deceived my eye and
                   judgment.

MARGARET   (moving quickly towards HERBERT)   No, I
                   should have demanded to see the king.   (She
                   goes down on to her knees.)   If I'd crawled at
                   his feet, shown him my suffering, he couldn't
                   have denied me. He'd have seen a mother begging
                   for her child and he'd have been moved. I should
                   have gone and knelt outside the palace gates until
                   he saw me.

HERBERT   (rising and raising MARGARET up)   My dear,
                   this is distraught fancy. You know well enough
                   there was nothing either of us could do. The
                   king isn't allowed to see the likes of us and, even
                   if he did, he is without power. The decisions lie
                   with men concerned with justice, not with
                   suffering.

MARGARET   (breaking away from HERBERT)   How can you
                   be so calm about it? How can you take it so
                   humbly, so passively? Even a brute beast would
                   fight, would show some sign of pain and passion.

HERBERT   (sitting)   I wish, Margaret, you could feel one
                   little part of my pain, as I believe I feel and
                   understand all of yours.

MARGARET   (sitting down)   There's a thought in my head
                   and I can't seem to quite catch it. I feel if I
                   could catch it and focus it, then everything would
                   be resolved. I must find that thought. I must.

HANGMAN   (rising, going D. S. , consulting watch again) I
                   have the feeling this train isn't going to be on
                   time. The service isn't what it was. Nothing is,
                   nothing is.   (Replaces watch in pocket.)

In this present case the victim was a whore,
(He pronounces it 'hoor'.)   one Lily-Ann
Turbett. A young woman, but, for all that, an
old whore. She'd been on the game even before
Nature made her ready for it. Given that she
wasn't much more than an animal, she wasn't
an unhandsome girl and, in other circumstances,
although she'd still have been a whore - that being
bred in the bone, so to speak - she could have
done quite well for herself. As it was, her
clients was mainly scum like herself.   (Again
consults watch and replaces it.)

MARGARET   I feel the thought has something to do with that -
                        that -

HERBERT   Hush, my dear, hush.

MARGARET   That creature.

HANGMAN   (moving back to the bench and sitting, he picks up
                        bag, opens it, takes out newspaper, closes bag,
                        puts it back down, opens newspaper, glances at
                        it, lowers it)   On the night of the event she
                        returned to her single room dwelling at ten p.m.,
                        having been out on the street for four hours. She
                        evidently returned alone. One Agnes Hooper, a
                        person of the same breed, who lived and plied her
                        trade in the room above Lily-Ann Turbett's,
                        reported that whilst she herself was on the way
                        down to the street -   (Mimicking.)   'I
                        always take a turn out in the air around about
                        that time of night' - laughter in court - she heard
                        Turbett shouting and screaming and beating on
                        the floor.

                        (LILY-ANN slowly rises to her knees and,
                        stooping over, thumps upon the stage.)

LILY-ANN   Stop your racket, you rotten bleeders, or I'll do
                        for you proper.

HANGMAN   Turbett was addressing the rats which infest the
                        premises.

LILY-ANN   Show yourselves and I'll bite your bleeding 'eads off, just see if I don't!

HANGMAN   Hooper left the house, but observed no one in the vicinity.

(LILY-ANN rises and, humming 'She's Only a Bird in a Golden Cage', goes and sits down in front of mirror.)

LILY-ANN   (peering into mirror)   Oh, my God, girl, you don't 'alf look rough.

HANGMAN   At some time between ten o'clock and midnight Claude Vole entered Lily-Ann Turbett's room.

(CLAUDE enters R. He carries a silver-mounted cane.)

HANGMAN   There being no evidence that he had ever visited Turbett on previous occasions, the inference is that he saw her whilst she was street-walking, recognised her for what she was and followed her home. Other whores have stated that this is quite a common occurence.

MARGARET   Why should he go to such a person?

HERBERT   It's too late to think on that now.

LILY-ANN   (turning round, coyly wagging finger)   Ain't you the bold one, coming right into a girl's room wifout as much as one little knock, eh? And me only in my wotsits!

CLAUDE   I - I -

LILY-ANN   (rising)   No matter. I'm not really put out. Just 'aving you on. Seen me in the street, did you?

CLAUDE   That's right. I was standing in the arcade by the wharf.

LILY-ANN   That's my stretch - that arcade.   (Posturing.) Took a fancy to what you seen, did you?

CLAUDE   Yes. Yes, indeed.

LILY-ANN   And why not? That's what it's there for.

                  (CLAUDE turns away D.S., then hesitates.
                  LILY-ANN bites upon lip.)

                  Not going already, surely?   (Pause.)
                  First time?

CLAUDE   (not looking at her)   No.

LILY-ANN   There ain't no 'urry, you know. Got all night
                  Leastways, I do.

HANGMAN   Claude Herbert Vole, aged twenty-three,
                  unmarried, unqualified music teacher and church
                  organist. Father: Herbert Vole, two hundred
                  pounds a year law clerk of twenty-five years
                  standing. Mother: Margaret Vole, one-time
                  school teacher who, as the saying goes, married
                  beneath her. Abode: a red brick semi-detached
                  house built in eighteen-eighty-one in a South
                  London suburb. To all intents and purposes the
                  entire Vole family was financially solvent and
                  morally respectable. People who kept themselves
                  to themselves, as decent people should.

LILY-ANN   I need the money and that's a fact.

                  (CLAUDE extends a hand sideways, palm open,
                  but he stares in front of him. LILY-ANN advances
                  and from CLAUDE's open palm picks up a coin.

LILY-ANN   A 'alf sovreign! Well!

                  (She holds CLAUDE's extended hand and lightly
                  traces on it with her index finger.)

                  What would you expect a girl to do for that kind of
                  money?   (Pauses.)   I don't do nothing funny -
                  nothing queer nor unnat'ral. I never 'ave and
                  'ope I never will.

HANGMAN   Hooper told the court that Turbett was a straight
                  whore, refusing to provide clients with any
                  sexual deviations. Like Hooper herself, she
                  regarded anything other than straight-forward

copulation as being highly immoral.

MARGARET   What did he look for from such an animal? What
            was in him that drove him to such an abomination?

HERBERT   Margaret, Margaret, he was a man and some men,
            many men - perhaps most men - carry a weight of
            terrible needs. They are needs they don't
            understand themselves and neither they, nor
            anyone else, can put names to them.

LILY-ANN   You ain't 'alf a quiet one and that's the truth.
            Don't come from round 'ere, do you?

            (CLAUDE shakes his head.)

            Didn't think so. Mostly seafaring men round 'ere
            and dockers. Very rough mostly. Just bang-
            bang wif them and then out of the door. Don't
            'ardly wait to take their 'ats off. Why don't you
            come and sit down a spell?

            (LILY-ANN leads CLAUDE U.S. where they sit
            on chairs in front of table. He puts his cane on
            the floor.)

            There, no sense putting weight on the bunions for
            no reason.

            (She has released his hand but now CLAUDE
            extends his hand again. LILY-ANN stares at
            him, puzzled, questioning, unsure, then takes
            his hand into hers.)

HANGMAN   After the veal and ham pie, I'll have rice pudding.
            Ye-esss, thick rice pudding with a golden skin to
            it and lots of fresh cream poured all over it.

            (MARGARET rises, embracing herself, as if
            cold.)

HERBERT   Are you cold?

            (MARGARET shakes her head 'No'. At this point
            action should freeze in all three sections of stage
            and should so continue for about thirty seconds.
            Then faintly and briefly there is the sound of a

<table>
<tr><td></td><td>single voice (male) singing some music hall air.)</td></tr>
<tr><td>CLAUDE</td><td>What's that?</td></tr>
<tr><td>LILY-ANN</td><td>Just someone going 'ome from the pub.</td></tr>
<tr><td>HERBERT</td><td>The milkman's singing.</td></tr>
<tr><td>MARGARET</td><td>What?</td></tr>
<tr><td>HERBERT</td><td>He always does.</td></tr>
<tr><td>CLAUDE</td><td>She demands of me more than I could ever give.</td></tr>
<tr><td>LILY-ANN</td><td>Who's this, then?</td></tr>
<tr><td>CLAUDE</td><td>She expects me to reach a height I know is far, far beyond me.</td></tr>
<tr><td>LILY-ANN</td><td>Are you all right, dearie?</td></tr>
<tr><td>CLAUDE</td><td>He knows I'm incapable of soaring high, but he doesn't do anything to stop her expecting miracles from me.</td></tr>
<tr><td>LILY-ANN</td><td>I shouldn't be surprised but it won't make no diff'rence a 'undred years from now, whatever it is as is worrying you. I always tell myself that. Lily-Ann girl, I say, it won't make a blind bit of diff'rence a 'undred years from now. There's a kind of comfort in that, there really is.</td></tr>
<tr><td>MARGARET</td><td>I took you for better or worse and didn't expect anything other than something equidistant between the two. But in him -   (Raises her hands to her mouth as if in prayer.)   oh, in him I reposed the very essence of myself, the very reason for my existence.</td></tr>
<tr><td>LILY-ANN</td><td>Do you want to do it, then?</td></tr>
<tr><td>CLAUDE</td><td>Do it? Yes.</td></tr>
<tr><td></td><td>(They rise. They stand face to face. With a sudden movement he kisses her very passionately.)</td></tr>
<tr><td>LILY-ANN</td><td>'Struth, but you ain't 'alf the funny one.</td></tr>
<tr><td>CLAUDE</td><td>Didn't it please you?</td></tr>
</table>

LILY-ANN   Please me? You've got it the wrong way round,
                guv. I ain't 'ere to be pleased. I'm the 'ore.

CLAUDE   (kissing her again)   Mother, mother darling,
                sweet and terrible mother.

LILY-ANN   (drawing back)   What's that? Look, mister, I
                said nothing unnat'ral and I meant it. What goes
                on in your 'ead's your business but just keep it
                there, see.

CLAUDE   Disapproval. Anger. Failed you. Don't
                measure up, don't meet your requirements, don't
                satisfy your demands.

LILY-ANN   Leave off that kind of talk. Fair gives me the
                creeps that way of going on.

CLAUDE   Oh, those disapproving eyes and those clamped
                lips.

LILY-ANN   If you ain't going to do nothing you might as well
                take your bleeding 'alf sovreign back and go,
                mister.

CLAUDE   Go? Go, you say? You'd never let me, never
                in a thousand years. I won't be free of you until
                I'm in my grave, or you're in yours.

LILY-ANN   Stop it! You just stop it, 'ear?

CLAUDE   One last kiss and it will be done. One last
                embrace and it is ended.

LILY-ANN   That's more like it. But you be'ave yourself,
                see?

                (CLAUDE kisses her again and then takes her
                neck between his hands. She utters a choking
                cry. She beats at him with her fists.)

MARGARET   (turning to look at HERBERT)   I have that
                thought.

HERBERT   What?

MARGARET   It was there in my mind all the time and I
                couldn't grasp at it.

HERBERT   You're distressing yourself, Margaret.

MARGARET   Listen. They need a life for that creature's.
                     What does it matter to them whose life it is? Let
                     them take mine.

HERBERT   Margaret.

MARGARET   I may as well be dead. A woman's life for a
                     woman's life. That's fair. After all, it's just a
                     kind of transaction. And he could live. Don't
                     you see, he could live and if he lived, why I'd be
                     living, too.

HERBERT   You poor unhappy woman.

MARGARET   Oh you! You never understand anything. You see
                     nothing, know nothing, think nothing. You're
                     empty nothingness, a great black vacuum.

                     (She turns towards C.S. LILY-ANN has slipped
                     to her knees. CLAUDE releases her and she
                     falls to stage. CLAUDE kneels by her.)

CLAUDE   Are you asleep?   (Sniffs.)   I know the
                     smell of you when you are asleep. Did you know
                     that? The smell of clean flesh. The smell of that
                     big bed. The smell of him upon you.

                     (HANGMAN rises, picks up his bag and goes to
                     C.S.)

MARGARET   (tunelessly)   Ride a cock-horse to Banbury
                     Cross,
                     To see a fine lady on a white horse,
                     Rings on her fingers, bells on her toes,
                     She shall have music wherever she goes.

                     (HERBERT rises and goes to MARGARET. He
                     puts an arm on her shoulder.)

HERBERT   My dear, you should go back to bed.

                     (HANGMAN, HERBERT and MARGARET now
                     stand at C.S. with backs to audience and
                     blocking CLAUDE and LILY-ANN from view.)

HANGMAN   A sexual act was performed upon the whore's
               corpse. Then Claude Herbert Vole ran from
               Lily-Ann Turbett's room. Outside the house he
               brushed against yet another whore, one Ida
               Laidlaw. She said: 'He bumped against me as I
               stood beneath the gaslight. The expression on his
               face was very terrible and I shan't forget it to
               the day I die.' The very next day, when it was
               discovered that bloody murder had been done, Ida
               Laidlaw described that face to an artist in the
               employ of the Globe Daily News and from the
               description an artistic impression was made and
               published in the newspaper. It led to the arrest of
               Claude Vole. From the moment of his arrest he
               refused point-blank to see his parents.

HERBERT   Margaret, if you won't go to bed at least come and
               sit down. You only weary yourself.

MARGARET   And why shouldn't I?

HERBERT   Come.

               (HERBERT leads MARGARET back to R. It is now
               seen that CLAUDE is kneeling, cradling LILY-
               ANN and kissing her. He lays her face down
               again and rises, turning his back on HANGMAN.
               CLAUDE puts his hands behind his back.)

MARGARET   (stopping)   It is almost time.

HERBERT   Yes.

MARGARET   It's a fearful thing he has to face alone.

HERBERT   He will have a chaplain and the word of God.

MARGARET   But still alone, all alone.

               (During the next speech, the HANGMAN puts his
               case upon the stage, opens it and from it
               withdraws straps with which he fastens CLAUDE's
               wrists. Then from the case he takes a canvas hood
               which he puts over CLAUDE's head and fastens at
               the back of his neck.)

HANGMAN   Vole could provide no alibi, nor could he give the
               police a satisfactory explanation for the presence
               at the scene of the crime of the silver-mounted
               cane. The cane - a gift from his ever-loving
               parents - was engraved with his initials and the
               date of his twenty-first birthday.

MARGARET   You went into the box and told them about the
               cane. You testified against your own flesh and
               blood.

HERBERT   I didn't testify against him, Margaret. I
               testified to the truth. The Law requires that of a
               man, no matter what. Besides -

HANGMAN   Besides, there was all them fingerprints.
               Devilishly incriminating things, fingerprints.
               Talk about the wonders of modern science! Even
               so, young Vole would not confess to the crime,
               maintaining that he had absolutely no recollection
               of the incident. His mind, so he said, was a
               complete blank. However, he was medically
               examined, declared sane and pronounced fit to
               stand trial. So tried he was by due process and
               was found guilty and was sentenced to hang by
               the neck until he be dead. Appeal was denied and
               reprieve withheld. Although urged to confess his
               guilt, he refused so to do to the very end.

MARGARET   Will he bear himself bravely?

HERBERT   God willing.

               (HANGMAN faces CLAUDE towards R. and
               slowly they begin to walk.)

HANGMAN   During his period of incarceration he was
               withdrawn but of moderately good cheer. On the
               short walk to the gallows, however, he suddenly
               displayed some signs of weakness. Indeed, the
               young man soiled himself. That can happen on
               these occasions. From the time he left the
               cell until the end he uttered one word alone, but
               this he repeated over and over again. It was -

CLAUDE   Mother.

                        (CLAUDE keeps repeating 'Mother' from now on.
                        HANGMAN takes CLAUDE to extreme R. and
                        faces him towards audience.)

MARGARET   The pains came at three o'clock in the morning.
                        I knew my time had come. I wakened Herbert
                        and he went to fetch the midwife. When the
                        midwife arrived the pains were very bad.
                        (Slides slightly down on her chair and puts her
                        legs apart. Speaks now with grunts and gasps.)
                        The midwife made things ready. She held my
                        hand. She told me how to - Oh, that was bad,
                        bad, bad! - How to bear down.   (Presses her
                        fingers upon her stomach with a downward
                        motion.)   The pains grew ever worse and I
                        felt sure I must soon breathe my last. I felt a
                        great anger against Herbert take possession of
                        me. Pain and anger and fear all cohesed. The
                        midwife tried to cheer me - how can I live through
                        this? - tried to cheer me by saying that the babe
                        must be a lusty boy, for no girl would ever be so
                        rough on her mama. Despite her joking I could
                        see from her eyes that she was afraid for my life.
                        So I continued until eight in the morning when
                        suddenly I felt as if my entire person was being
                        torn apart and fragmented and being flung into
                        empty space. I - I - called out -

                        (A clock strikes eight. HERBERT puts one hand to
                        his throat.)

CLAUDE   (very loudly and, through the muffling of the hood,
                        almost like a beast's cry of pain)   Mother!

MARGARET   (screaming)   My baby!

                        (Instant black out at stage R. HERBERT opens the
                        bible and rises to his feet.)

HERBERT   (in a very firm voice)   Woman, get to your
                        knees. We have a son's soul to pray for.

                        (Momentarily MARGARET stares at HERBERT,

then quietly rises and then goes down upon her
knees. HERBERT also kneels.)

(Reading from the bible.)   Let not your heart
be troubled: ye believe in God, believe also in
me. In my Father's house are many mansions, if
it were not so I would have told you. I go to
prepare a place for you. And if I go and prepare
a place for you, I will come again and receive you
unto myself; that where I am, there ye may be
also. And whither I go ye know and the way ye
know.

MARGARET   Amen.

(They rise and with HERBERT supporting
MARGARET they exit L. Stage L. blacks out.
HANGMAN comes to C. and packs straps and hood
back into Gladstone bag, which he closes and
then picks up.)

HANGMAN   When the whore Turbett was found dead they had to
force open one fist and discovered that she
clutched a half sovereign. Nasty lot is whores.
(Consults watch.)   That's the train now.
Exactly one and one-half minutes late. I've a
good mind to write a letter of formal complaint to
the company. Although I don't expect it would do
me any good. Nothing's as it was.

(He exits R. There is a knocking sound as if upon
a door. From off stage a female voice is heard:
'Lily-Ann, is you up? Agnes here. Any chance
of borrowing a little bit of sugar, girl?
(Pause.)   Lily-Ann? Lily-Ann?   (Pause.)
Oh, my God!   (Pause.)   Oh, my bleeding
God!' There is an enormous scream.

Instant fade at stage C.)